There's Men EVERYWHERE

If You Lower Your Standards!

Dr. Zelda Bing

There's Men EVERYWHERE

Tired of looking for Mr. Right?
Are you ready to look for
Mr. "Oh... All Right!?"

Dr. Zelda Bing

Cool Jerk Publishing

There's Men Everywhere © November 2015
by Dr. Zelda Bing

DR. KNOW-IT-ALL-PUBLISHING / Cool Jerk Publishing

11433 Rochester Ave. Suite # 302

Los Angeles, CA 90025

For information visit: www.zeldabing.com

Book and Cover design by: Buddy Bing

ISBN-13: 978-0692532560

First Edition, Cool Jerk Publishing: November 2015

Dedication

To: Me, I did it...

...and Paul Lyons, Arlene Schindler, Cathy
Ladman, Sheila Kay, and of course, Pat
Sierchio, without whom Zelda would not exist.

Your Life Is About To Be Transformed...

(Better Go Grab A Cookie To Go With It.)

WARNING:

THIS BOOK WON'T FIND YOU A MAN.
YOU ARE EVENTUALLY GOING
TO HAVE TO LEAVE THE HOUSE.
- DR. ZELDA BING

.

Contents

Foreword

When Zelda insisted that I write this forward, I gulped with insecurity, aloud like a cartoon character. "What if she's disappointed? What if it *sucks?*"

Sound crazy? Maybe, since she is my alter ego. But Zelda gets what Zelda wants. So here we go...

Hard to believe that out of me, came Zelda; like a dwarf giving birth to a giant, because she's way more together than I am. I was working on a show that poked fun of self-help, and she literally just *popped out* one day. This hideous woman with her strange ticks had the confidence I craved, the self-esteem I only dreamed about and the gall I lacked. Men dug her, women wanted to be her. Trust me, men go crazy, even ga-ga for her. Me? Not so much. And let's face it I am prettier, and way thinner. (I am too!) It's complicated. Let's face it, it's hard being a woman. Or as Zelda says, "If it were easy

being a women more men would do it too."
Or did Debbie say that? Stay with me...

Although I tease the self-help culture, I've
always had a shelf full of new-age books
written by the hippest gurus du jour. But the
only thing they ever really helped was my
shelves. I struggled for decades dealing with
the opposite sex, always trying to find a
piece of some happy. It wasn't until Zelda
Bing burst into my life, and showed me how
to take what I wanted, that things started
falling into place. She dishes out great
advice like, "Love yourself, just not in front
of anybody." And "Younger men make much
better lovers ... their life stories are much
shorter."

Zelda believes you can have what you want,
just by believing it. So Zelda believes she's
the Homecoming Queen in the football game
of life. She's confident, sexy, and in control
of her destiny. Zelda has completed me. She
can fill in your missing pieces too. And
maybe add a few parts that you didn't even
know were missing. (If you play your cards,
right she may even let you borrow her
dress!) Her tools work; I have a boyfriend
now, finally. Of course he loves Zelda more

than he loves me, but we're working through that! Open yourselves up to the Zelda Bing experience and all things can be yours. (Just don't leave her alone with your men.)

This satire offers many genuine truths I have stumbled across (or extrapolated) along the way. Her advice is timely, and not just about men. She has plenty to say about women and everyone else, too. Please take Zelda how she is intended; with tongue planted firmly in check. But dammit, she's always right! If I were you, I would heed her advice as if your life depended on it.

Please enjoy Zelda, I certainly do.

Debbie Kasper

Puppet to Zelda

Introduction

By Zelda Bing

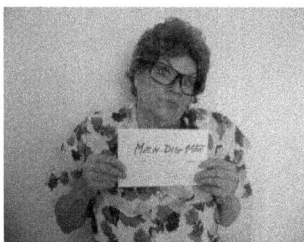

What can I say? Men dig me. I am a man-magnet. I couldn't stop them if I wanted to. I've got that *Je-nay-say-qua* (1). Pardon my French. I don't brag, I simply state facts. But fret not, I've written this book to spread my "*qua*" around. (2) This **MAN**-ual will help you wade your way through the deep and crappy end of the sewer plant of love. In other words, I'm going to help you locate, identify and hold onto a man. Because, let's face it, keeping him is the hard part. It's easy to find someone to sleep with you. The hard part is getting him to sleep with you *again,* and forever and always. *(Oh my goodness, that sounds almost life-threatening, doesn't it?)*

Even a Pet Rock Came with an Instruction Manual!

Scout's honor, when it comes to men, without a guidebook, you might as well be a sperm trying to swim its way through a vasectomy. Eventually you hit that darn wall.

Isn't it high time you got off your high horse and learned to settle, missy? And I think I know a little something about men—I've been married four times (although once was by accident... I thought we were doing a play)!

We will talk about forever, later. Much later. Like, never.

NOBODY CAN MAKE
A MAN LOVE YOU!
BUT THIS BOOK DOES
GIVE YOU THE TOOLS
TO STALK HIM & HUNT HIM DOWN
UNTIL EVENTUALLY
HE TIRES OF RUNNING!

This is the last book about men you'll <u>ever</u> have to buy. Mind you, men don't have manuals on us *chicki-wahs* (3). They don't surf the Kindle Sea looking for books on how different men and women are. They don't care. I asked some. They just think we're strange. We think that comment needs delving into, whereas men really only like to delve into *us*. Seriously, ladies, why aren't there books telling men how to catch US??! I wrote one, and it sold ONE COPY ... to my brother, Zeke Bing. And he's gay. Actually, I had to buy it for him because he's broke, too. (Don't tell him I told you.)

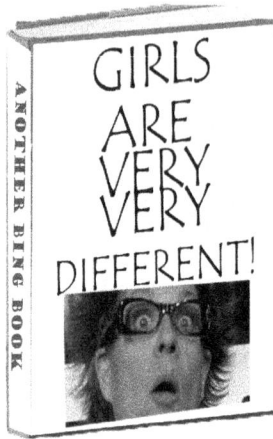

Here are some book titles for men you'll never see:

- ♥ Broads Are People Too (In a Way)
- ♥ Wanna Hold My Drink While I Take A Wicked Piss? (& Other Snappy Pick-up Lines)
- ♥ 50 Shades of Beer
- ♥ Hot Chicks & Other Pizza Toppings
- ♥ Men Who Run with the Bitches
- ♥ How to Keep Your Babe from Going Lesbo
- ♥ Chicks! One More Thing I Gotta Friggin' Worry About

Men believe a fat wad of cash and a bucketful of spicy chicken wings are the only self-help they will ever need—for *anything.* Furthermore, they think if you bother to read a "how to" book, you better have a free-standing wood shed at the end to show for it.

**AND IF YOU THINK THAT'S
A STEREOTYPE, READ ON—
THAT'S JUST THE BEGINNING.
THIS BOOK IS CHOCK FULL OF THEM!**

Hence, we the chicki-wahs, are in charge of the relationships. We are the **Mating Butlers** (4). That's right; if love were grass, we'd be the mower. If love were an eyebrow, we'd be the pluckers. It's only page eleven, and already I digress. We women do that. We like to go off on tangents; we unpack bags, decorate, and stay awhile. We even throw a tangent party and invite our friends. Men can't follow tangents.

Hello? Men? Yoo-hoo? Yodel-lay-he-who?!

See? I've lost them. Radio silence. They're like dogs at a squirrel sanctuary. But, getting back to my point that men don't read about, ask for, or want help. They have it all worked out that women do all the work. We read all the books, and we go on all the diets, while they go out for spicy wing-dings at the beer saloon with another Mr. Man-hole who isn't worrying about women, either.

We chicki-wahs stay home, popping **Garcinia Cambogia (5)** tablets and running on the treadmills that lurk in our bedrooms (acting like clothes hangers). Just so our skin will fit us nicely should one of them ask to see us in the buff!

This is not a self-help book, or as I prefer to call them, *shelf-help books*, because they fill up your shelves, not your life.

*This is a **zelf-help book**. It's help for your new zesty-self,* your "**ZELF**"(6). By the end of this guidebook, you'll have a plan, a blueprint for happiness for your zelf. Besides, a book won't find you a man, but going fishing will. So, this zelf-help book will help you get some tools to teach you how to swim in the swamp of love. Consider this book a pair of flippers, if you will.

**THIS ISN'T A HOBBY,
IT'S A JOB!
HOLD YOUR NOSE AND
DIVE INTO THE DEEP END!**

Part I:
Why Be Alone And Miserable When You Can Be Miserable With Someone?

The sad but true fact is that beautiful, glorious women everywhere are date-free, alone, untethered, unloved, and sobbing in dark cafes over a split of wine *(that they split with themselves)*. I can only imagine that men are alone, too; but we don't hear men bitching that they can't find girls. Men don't complain much, period. They don't like to complain because it might be misinterpreted as communication. Men don't like to communicate; it gets in the way of the sex. Women, on the other hand, love to complain. To us gals, complaining is foreplay (much, much more on complaining as communication in PART IV).

WOMEN BELIEVE THAT COMPLAINING BURNS CALORIES. THAT'S WHY THIN WOMEN ARE SO BITCHY.

From all corners of the world, you can hear women whine that there just aren't any men anywhere. Boo-hoo. Every time I hear a chicki-wah say, "I can't find a man, boo-hoo!", I know right off the bat that she just doesn't use her peepers. I know. I used to be that chicki-wah! Zelda Bing spent an entire decade, single in Akron, Ohio, whining that I never met any men, like a starving orangutan in a library, crying, *"Where's all the bananas?"* Then I got hip to the scene, man. You must go where they are.

(BTW, the only men who came into my apartment that decade in Akron were Chinese food delivery boys. Honest, you can bolt the door behind them all you want, and weep, "I'm so lonely!", and they still aren't going to marry you! They have other Moo-Goo-Gai-Pans (7) to deliver.

There are men everywhere. So, if you can't find one, possibly something else is going on with you; like maybe, perhaps, deep down inside, you're just not ready. Maybe YOU can't cope with the schtuff a relationship might leave on your door step. Possible?

Yes, having a relationship with a man is like having a job, but every day is Monday. You need to have patience, tools, help, and ice cream. If you can't cope, you can't cope. It's not for everybody.

MY VERY OLD GREAT AUNT PHOEBE ALWAYS SAID, "COPE, SCHMOPE, PASS THE SCOTCH" (THAT'S AN OPTION, TOO).

A man will make you feel. That is a given. Feelings are work. So, yes, do the math— men are work. Maybe you're simply not ready to feel your feelings. Yes, feelings can hurt. **DOY! That's why they're called feelings.** Otherwise, they would be called candy. And if you're not up for the task, it's not required. You do not need a man to complete you. You are already complete. It's vital that at this exact point in time, to make sure you are up for this.

But, if you really want one, then read on (but don't say Zelda didn't warn you. Seriously, don't. Seriously).

The point is:

Stop Waiting For A Man To Complete You.

Complete Yourself, Yourself.

Most Importantly:

BE YOURSELF. BE YOU. YOURSELF.

No One Else Wants The Job, Trust Me.

I'm not that kind of girl... I'm the other kind

Have You Been Single So Long You Pick Fights With Your Handyman?
(Just To Remember What It Was Like To Be In Love?)

Before I became the man-magnet that I am, I was once single for so long I dreamt about my eighth-grade boyfriend. Except in my dream he was still in the eighth grade, and I didn't give a toad's stool.

**YOUNGER MEN MAKE
MUCH BETTER LOVERS.
THEIR LIFE STORIES
ARE MUCH SHORTER.**

When you're single too long, you begin to lose hope, and your loins stop crying out. It is time to get back on the track, and get those loins making meow sounds again.

Here are some hints that you've been single too long:

- ♥ *You call the Jehovah's Witnesses to ask where they've been.*
- ♥ *The weatherman predicts eight inches, and you put on perfume.*
- ♥ *Your vibrator is filing for disability.*
- ♥ *Your own mother called you 'gay.'*

WARNING:
YOU ARE ABOUT TO WALK THROUGH SOME HOT, HOT COALS!

This quiz will help you decide if you are ready to partner up.

Are You Ready For A Boyfriend? Quiz:

Can you hold your hand over an open flame and not whimper?

A. Yes.
B. No.
C. I've been practicing!

Are you ready to pretend like you care who wins the Superbowl this year?

A.   Yes.
B.   No.
C.   What's a Superbowl?

Are you ready to have this question answered: "Do these shoes make my ass look fat?" (Even if you didn't ask!)

A.   No.
B.   Not on a bet.
C.   Can't I date a gay man?

Do you enjoy watching LIFETIME? Because those days are OVER, BABY!

(This is a rhetorical question; if you even tried to answer, you are NOT ready).

RESULTS: *If you answered C to ANY of the above questions... You are not ready! If you answered A to all the questions, then read on… You are ready. If you failed miserably, then go back to page one. Start over. Meditate. Buy another of these books. Send a few to your friends. Get a pet or a plant, but you are NOT READY for a human or a man. Keep your plants alive for five days in a row, and then move up to a pet.*

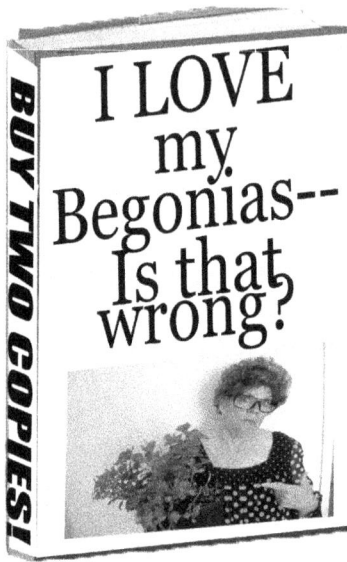

I LOVE my Begonias-- Is that wrong?

BUY TWO COPIES!

Meet your new boyfriend!

(This boyfriend doesn't mind if you accidentally lock him outside for the night. He also doesn't care if you blow off his birthday; he will still lick you!)

LOVE YOURSELF: It's a Dirty Job—But Someone's Gotta Do It!

The first person you need to love is... YOU! Remember all those dumb old mothers, aunts, and grandmothers who told you that if you don't love yourself, nobody will love you either? They were right! Love begins with **you.** You may even discover that you are the man of your dreams! You could be the **YOU,** you're looking for! Seriously, maybe you are your own soulmate! Take yourself out, have your way with you. Learn to master-date!

AFFIRMATION:
"I LOVE ME SO MUCH,
I AM MY OWN BOYFRIEND!"

We all suffer from a touch of the low self-esteem influenza. I call it an influenza because it can spread and it can linger; and the only thing that tastes good while under its spell are chocolate chip cookies.

All humans have low self-esteem. That's what separates us from other mammals. We are the only members of our food group who judge themselves. Have you ever seen an elephant at the zoo say, "Excuse me, does my ass look fat?" No! They eat peanuts like there's no tomorrow. Dogs have more self-esteem than we do. Watch a dog sometime. They'll walk up to a complete stranger and lick them. Can you do that? I won't do that … ever again. (This, BTW, does not attract a man to you. Most men do NOT enjoy being licked—*in public).*

The reason you have such low self-esteem is because the earliest form of human life is thought to be bacteria, which means:

Your ancestors could have been a yeast infection.

Be careful what you think of yourself; I'm just sayin'.

THE SUBCONSCIOUS IS ALL—POWERFUL. IT KNOWS EVERYTHING. IT'S WORSE THAN THE NSA!

REMEMBER THIS: You are what you think—you think what you feel. So, why not feel like a Zelda Bing? I am a man-magnet. I couldn't stop it if I wanted to, but I repeat myself, we women do repeat ourselves, a lot. Men say things ONCE, so you better be within earshot.

You know, I used to not love myself. That's right, I'm not just a counselor—I'm a client. My self-esteem used to be so low, I wrote my autobiography, and I wasn't even in it. I spent most of my life caring more about what YOU thought of me than what I thought of me.

Good ol' Great-Aunt Phoebe always used to say, "You wouldn't care so much what others thought of you if you knew how seldom they did."

**MY SELF-ESTEEM USED TO BE SO LOW,
ONE TIME A MAN
CALLED ME
THE WRONG NAME IN BED,
AND I GAVE HIM THREE MORE GUESSES.**

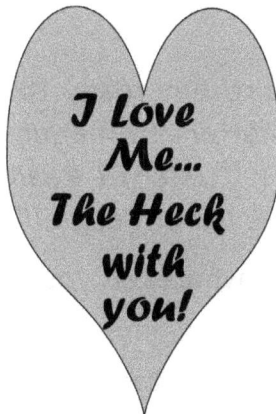

I Love Me... The Heck with you!

Earth to Subconscious!
(or Becoming The Wizard of ID)

The quickest way to self-love is to affirm it. You can have or be anything you want by affirming it. An affirmation is a positive statement made in a positive and present way. For example, if you say, "I think I'll clean out this mold-bin of a house today." Dollars to donuts, before you know it, you'll have a bottle of Tidy Bowl in your hands. So, an affirmation is merely a thought with an ax to grind. It is a goal with an expiration date.

IT'S THAT SIMPLE!

Try this affirmation. Say it to yourself: *"I Love You!"*

If you find you're not ready to say, "I love you," try this starter affirmation. Look into a mirror and say: *"Listen, I Really Like You— But I Wanna See Other People!"*

Why not affirm whatever you want in your life?

"Men dig me. They do too!"

Close your eyes, say that three times, and click your heels.

Now, say this:

"I'm buying more of these books and giving them to all my girlfriends this year. In fact, I'll take hundreds. I'll send them to strangers."

The previous affirmation actually works on two levels. Firstly, it starts you on your path to spirituality. Secondly, it helps with my personal goal of making this book a bestseller. Thank you.

Now get NIKE about it and JUST DO IT!

Most women aren't beautiful models from the cover of a magazine. Most of us are beautiful in our own way (or not), and you know which ones you are. But it's an inside job.

I'm prettier than I look!

Congratulations, now that you do affirmations, you have added spirituality to your arsenal of weapons.

You are tapped into the universe. Take a look around, and enjoy the view from up there.

So, affirmations are a way of talking to your subconscious (SC). Your SC is very powerful. It knows EVERYTHING. It's your personal NSA, but it has no sense of humor. It doesn't know when you're kidding.

Your SC doesn't understand irony, sarcasm, whining, nuances, tone of voice, or men. Honest! So you can't even joke around when it comes to your happiness. If you say things like, "Men don't dig me!", it becomes a self fufilling prophecy. Perhaps you'll walk around with food between your teeth or boogers hanging out of your nose. You may do stupid things in front of him. You'll self-sabotage it. *So be very careful what you say and think.*

What Is Love?

I'm A Doctor, Dammit!

So These Are Not Opinions, They Are Facts!

Love is relative (just don't date one).

There was even a song written about it that goes:

"If you can't be with the one you love— love the one you're with!"

How many of you are reading this *MAN-ual* to find love? *(BTW, anybody who doesn't admit they're looking for love is a big fat liar, liar, pants on fire).* We all want love. Even snakes seek warmth and comfort!

"FALLING IN LOVE IS LIKE DROPPING ACID. IT MAY BE GOOD, IT MAY BE BAD, BUT WHEN IT'S OVER— NO MUSIC WILL EVER SOUND THE SAME AGAIN!"

-Anonymous (French for "stolen from the internet")

You have to give love to get love, and the source of love is YOU—so start pumping out some love! Love is a feeling that is so unbelievably all-encompassing and gooey, it doesn't really matter who you share it with. Who you are in love with is neither here nor there. We all just want to be gooey all over. Love can melt, so be warned: Do NOT leave it out in the hot sun (much more about love later on in this manual. Much, much more).

Many people think love is supposed to be firecrackers and heart palpitations, so they spend their lives disappointed. As Aunt Phoebe always said:

**THE ROAD TO DISAPPOINTMENT
IS LITTERED WITH EXPECTATIONS!
EXPECT NOTHING--
YOU'LL NEVER BE DISAPPOINTED.**

So—What is Love, Anyway? Yeah! What Is It?

So, perhaps it's time to define l-o-v-e. I'm a doctor, and I barely know—and I've studied this. Is it a feeling? A thought? An emotion? An idea? A duty? A need? A want? A hope? A wish? Does love really make the world go 'round? Is love REALLY all you need? Is love really never having to say you're sorry? Yeah, for the MEN!

FALLING IN LOVE IS WHAT SEPARATES US FROM OTHER MAMMALS. WE FALL IN LOVE— THEY ROLL AROUND IN IT.

If music is the food of love—then pig out!

Yes, love is a many splendored thing—I believe that love is a song we sing—I might as well face it, I'm addicted to love. So go ahead and love, love me do—love me two times—love me like a rock. But some say love is like a river that drowns the tender reed—I don't care what they say, I won't stay in a world without love. Sooner or later love is gonna get you. Sooner or later, love is gonna win because—Everybody loves somebody sometime, and your sometime is now.

Yes, there are many kinds of love...

There's baby love, young love, stoned love, groovy kind of love. There's a hunka-hunka burning love and muskrat love! There's when the moon hits your eye like a big pizza pie-kinda love too—that's amoré!

Don't you want somebody to love? Don't you need somebody to love? You better find somebody to love—You've got to live a little, take a little, and let your poor heart break a little. Play the game of love. Because the purpose of a man is to love a woman, and the purpose of a woman is to love a man. Come on baby, let's start to play. Hello, I love you; won't you tell me your name, treat me like a fool, treat me mean and cruel, but love me. Don't break my heart, my achy breaky heart—You made me love you, I didn't wanna do it. I didn't wanna do it—I'm gonna make you love me, you're my prisoner of love, and you're gonna love me like nobody's loved me, come rain or come shine—and one way or another, I'm gonna getcha, getcha, getcha, getcha—one way or another—every step you take, every move you make, I'll be watching you—can't you see you belong to me? So just STOP in the name of love cause I'm crazy—crazy for feeling so blue. HELP, I need somebody! They're coming to take me away, ha ha! They're coming to take me away, ho-ho-hee-hee, ha-ha! To the funny farm where life is beautiful all the time, and I'll be happy to see those nice young men in their clean white coats, and they're coming to take me AWAYYYYYYYY!... Ha-ha, ho-ho to the funny farm. That's the story of, that's the glory of love (breathe).

The Law Of The Universe – Ying & Yang Along

Yes, love hurts. Get over it, Ms. Wimpy-doodle! Anything that feels good also feels bad at some point.

If I wanted my feelings hurt... I would've called my mother!

It's the law of the universe. It's the "what goes up must come down" syndrome. You have to take the ying with the yang. One man's pain is another man's gain. One man's art is another man's fart. One man's … oh well, you get the picture.

Part II:
Lower Your Standards, One Of Every Two People Is A Man!

Eeny-Meeny-Miney-Moe, Larry & Curly!

There are, quite simply, men everywhere. Look out your window, chicki-wah! If you see no men there, find another window and look out. Here's some men who need love: the butcher, the baker, and the candlestick maker. Let me repeat: There are men everywhere. Change your mind about what a man should look like.

If you think you are too good for the man pictured above, think again; and then go back to PAGE ONE. *You have missed Zelda's point.*

Waiting For Your Prince And Other Procrastinations

There are no princes (Prince is spaghetti).

Say that three more times. This isn't an affirmation; it's just a fact.

"There are no princes. There are no princes. There are no princes."

Get it? Even the artist formerly known as Prince isn't really a prince. It's all a fairytale.

And even if one did come along, why would he choose you? Not that there's anything wrong with you. I'm sure you are fairly apt. Again, I ask, are you sure you are ready for the adventure? Because dating is like tackling the wildest rollercoaster at an amusement park; it's the high-tracks ride. It gives you the butterflies-in-the-stomach effect.

The Scary Relationship Ride

To get on the ride, you have to wait in a long, hot line to prove your mettle; and then you have to pass the little "see if you're big enough" test. By the time you get in a car and they strap you in, your heart begins to palpitate. *You start having buyer's remorse, but you can't get out of the car because it's starting to move now. YIKES! So, there you are, chugging up a hill, you're kind of excited—but still pretty nervous, and paranoid. You look around, and by the time you get to the very tippy-top, you scream, "Somebody please punch me in the face if I even look like I might ever do this again!" After you arrive back at the loading station— where there's several other people waiting in line, you scream out randomly, "Don't do it! Run for your lives!"*

LOVE AIN'T FOR SISSIES!

Just What Is A Man?

Yes, what exactly IS a man!? They are of the same genus as women, but not really—in the way that mushrooms are of the fungus group, which means mushrooms and mold are in the same family. So it goes to reason, men are the toadstools of the *Homo sapiens* family. They're just weirdos. I really don't know how else to categorize them. And I love men, deeply and often. I don't like mushrooms, but I do love men. But they are weirdos. Repeat that so you really get how true that point is:

"Men are just weirdos!"

Spread it around. Heck, call a friend and tell her, too. It's a fact, jack. Men are wired differently; they think differently; they feel differently; and they look differently. Some have facial hair. Most have ear hair. Some have hair on their butts. It's pretty gross.

BTW, if you are a woman with ear hair or butt hair, this may NOT be the book for you. And getting a man might not be your biggest problem. I'm just sayin'! Get up and go to a barber (and barbers are generally men)!

*Men are
wired
wierd !*

41

So What Makes Men So Weird? Huh?!?!

Heck if I know! Just back off with the hounding questions. It's not like I'm a microbiologist, although I did once play "hide the specimen" with one.

There are boatloads of books out there outlining the differences between men and women:

- ❤ Men/Women WTF G-D?
- ❤ Men Speak Chinese, Women Like Puppies
- ❤ Men Are From Mars—Women Wish They Would Go Back There!
- ❤ Even If I Understood You, I Still Wouldn't Care

I've read them all, and sadly it seems the only thing men and women have in common is that we have nothing in common. And we're both carbon-based life forms. I do know one thing—we all worship the same thing: HIM. Remember that, and you'll be fine.

John Gray didn't make a gazillion bucks talking about women being from Venus and men being from Mars for no reason. I personally think the difference is vaster than two separate planets. If men are from Mars, then women are—nutcrackers. We are very different. So, what is the difference? Heck, if I knew that, I'd be John Gray.

First of all, men are self-centered. In fact, they are so self-centered, during sex, they sometimes call out their OWN names. Often they're alone, so they'd be correct. They're the center of their own universe; the president of their personal fan clubs; and the skipper of their little dinghies.

So, if you want a man, you must convince him that **you love him as much as he loves himself.** I am a man-magnet because I love them, and they know it. They can smell my adulation. I adulate loudly and often around men.

You have to learn to make the OHMIGAWD—You're-the-most-fabulous-thing-since-fat-free-yogurt face.

Here's what that looks like close-up:

Most men don't know what the heck they want. Seriously, they need a woman to tell them what they want. If it were left up to them, they'd still be sitting on rocks, eating prehistoric roadkill (raw). We are the ones who suggested cooking it! We came up with bowls, sauces, couches, paintings, spoons, and Toni home permanents. What did they come up with? Bowling balls, mud wrestling, and Hooters! Seriously!

Here are where your affirmations come in. Start with this one:

"You want me!"

That's right. Just approach, and say that.

As a single unit, and under no woman's influence, a man will listen to his idiotic beer

32332332

buddies who behave like circus seals when they are together. They're all listening to the little play they put on in front of each other, which never gets performed in front of ladies.

They can make an entire meal out of Velveeta and hot peppers; they laugh at fart jokes; they are not dateable in this pack-pool hall personality. They all want good-lookin' babes with long hair and a tight bottom (these same men voted for the chicken wing to become the state bird of Florida). You have to separate him from the pack and affirm him until he gives in.

**"MEN ARE LIKE A FINE WINE.
IT'S OUR JOB TO STOMP ON THEM AND
KEEP THEM IN A BARREL
UNTIL THEY MATURE INTO SOMETHING
YOU'D LIKE TO
HAVE DINNER WITH."**

-Anonymous

Trust me, I'm a doctor (have I mentioned this?), and men have no pea-picking idea what the heckola they want, or what they are. The thought that they want what they can't have is not true. Playing hard to get is a game; don't go there! It attracts the kind of man who only likes the hunt. You want a man to not only hunt you, but skin you and eat you.

Here Are Some Basic Differences Between Men & Women:

- ♥ Men don't know where you keep the vacuum (even if you tell them, the next time, they won't remember, again).

- ♥ Women are interested in other people's lives; men are interested in other women.

- ♥ Men knock things over when they walk; women pick the things up.

- ♥ Women will hand you a tissue when you're crying. If a man sees you crying, he might ask, "Is something wrong?" But, he will then quickly follow it up with a glance at his watch and ask, "Will this take much longer? I'm hungry."

Here Are Some Basic Similarities Between Men & Women:

- ❤ We both like to talk about HIM.
- ❤ We both like to eat food.
- ❤ We both think that the other is strange.
- ❤ We both announce it when we are going to the bathroom.
- ❤ We both are glad that we are not the other sex.
- ❤ We both find the questions on JEOPARDY to be hard.
- ❤ We both think the other is strange (oh, did I mention that one already?).

Finding These Men—Turning Over Rocks And Other Techniques

There are men everywhere. One out of every two people is a man. That means that every other person on this planet is a man. So, if you're not a man, then there's a good chance there's one really near you. In fact, you can probably pinch him he's so close.

(BTW, don't pinch him, it might frighten him. That's just a figure of speech.)

But do grab him. He may have a ring on his finger, so what? If he's alive, he's fair game.

Nothing is forever, except cellulite and the Columbia Record Club. (I joined once in the '70s, and I still get albums in the mail. *Are the Bee Gees even still together?*)

The best place to find a man in any town in America is driving in your car. If you see one walking down the street, just ... **hit him**. It's a great ice-breaker, and you know he'll ask for your number. Sure, my insurance is very high—but I write it off, and my tax consultant is cute as a button!

MEN ARE LIKE DOGS. IF A DOG SEES ANOTHER DOG PEEING, THEY WANT TO PEE THERE, TOO!

If a man sees another man dating you, he wants to date you too (or pee on you)! Let us learn from the mammals. Do you think llamas are picky who they play "hide the brisket" with? No. They mate with whoever smells good. Some end up with the ugly ones. There aren't enough pretty llamas to go around, but they're all happy just to find love. The hideous three-toed sloth even has a boyfriend. Sure, he's a baboon, but at least he is still hanging around.

What are you waiting for? Where's your baboon? There are plenty of them swinging in the trees! Why are you still sitting here reading? Go get some ice cream—there might be some man-e-os in line at the grocery store, or behind the counter at the ice cream stand.

WARNING!
DON'T SHOP FOR HAMMERS AT A FRUIT STAND. IF THERE ARE NO MEN WHERE YOU ARE...LEAVE!

(BTW: do NOT go get frozen yogurt, in hopes of meeting a man there. There are no men there.)

You will find only skinny bitches measuring out exactly four grams of fat-free yogurt, clogging up the joint, tasting every single flavor before they make up their mind, and getting their frequent visitor card punched. These are not our people.

Other places you will NOT FIND A MAN:

- ♥ **The maternity ward** – He's taken. He's just had a baby. Wow, take the hint!

- ♥ **The Gynocologist's office** – even if the Doctor is a man, you do not want to date a Gyno... Why? Because all women look alike to him.

- ♥ **Family reunion** – I know your cousin's cute. So is mine. Get over it.

- ♥ **Your apartment** – if he's already in your apartment and you are not having sex ... something is wrong.

Network, Footwork, Twitter, Glitter, Facebook, or Rot.

The truth is, love is a business and you're the product. You're a carton of milk with an expiration date and you're about to go sour; so, it's time to advertise. Put the word out. Write a personal ad, make a flyer, and start a multilayered marketing scheme. Make love a business. Call your friends—ask your friends to call their friends. Ask your friend's friends to call their friend's friends. And they'll tell two friends, and so on, and so on, and so on, and so on. This tactic worked for a shampoo commercial in the '70s, and it can work for you.

Get on Facebook, and reconnect with old boyfriends (yours or anybody's). Tweet, blog, Google, giggle, finagle, get a bagel, flirt with the counter boy. You will eventually have to leave your computer and go out, so when you do, open your eyes and remember the one-in-two rule! Send out some random sex-texts to some random men in your phone (just to get the juices flowing).

PUT AN AD ON CRAIGSLIST.
HECK, DATE CRAIG!
I HEAR HE'S SINGLE,
AND HE'S GOT THAT NICE LIST,
SO IF IT DOESN'T WORK OUT WITH HIM,
MAYBE HE'LL KNOW SOMEONE!

Join a dating website. Use this as your bio: "I'm not perfect. Seriously, if I were, I wouldn't be trolling on this site. But I'm gonna love you like nobody's loved you, come rain or come shine."

Stay away from the following dating sites:

- ❤ Lonely&Bitter.comski
- ❤ Stalkers@icu.com
- ❤ Mammasboy@cling-on.com
- ❤ Beggarsandchoosers@comover
- ❤ Shrewsontheprowl.comandgetme

I personally know several chicki-wahs who are engaged, married, living with, or already divorced from men they met on a dating website. They all did it the same way:

They posted pictures of themselves from 30 years and 30 pounds ago, and then met in a dimly lit place, for a full year, wearing a muumuu or a caftan. This works! By the time he realizes she's 50 and dumpy, he's trapped. Love is relative (but don't date one, that's icky).

More Places To Find Men

Be inventive—use your tools—grab your hammer!

- ❤ Get a job at the men's department in Macy's, and fold the shirts constantly while you smile at men in the aisle.
- ❤ Volunteer at a fire station and keep touching the pole and winking.

♥ Get a dog, take it for a walk, and let him lick everyone! Then you join in.

♥ Call a cab—when he picks you up, jump in the back seat with all your things and say "Just drive" (don't get out till the meter explodes).

♥ Stand in front of cheesy motels and flag down a man saying, "Excuse me, mister, could you help me find my puppy? I think he just ran into that cheap motel!"

♥ Stick your head into a strip mall go-go bar I guarantee you, you look better than most of the naked chicks on the pole.

♥ Heck, get your own pole and carry it around with you. Spin on it on street corners!

♥ Check into a hospital—doctors are good catches. Have something removed so you can stay a few days. You can afford to lose the following organs: **Spleen, tonsils, appendixes, gall bladders, one kidney, and some skin***

*Consult a physician before embarking on this plan.

Flirting, Hooking, Winking & Closing

So you say you can FIND a man, but now you don't know how to engage him in a conversation? Don't worry. He won't notice, and I mean that in the nicest possible way. Conversation is NOT what he's checking out.

If your technique is to keep looking at him, hoping he notices and comes over, forget it, sister. Other chicki-wahs know how to close the deal. It's time to step up to the plate and swing. It's time to get serious. Remember, love is a business.

Possible Scenarios:

Say you're driving on a highway, and you stink at driving. There's a guy on your butt, honking, flipping you the bird. Do you let him pass? NO! Flip him the bird back (that's foreplay in New Jersey). This is a meet. Flag him down, and wave him to pull over.

Say you're at a sporting event, there's probably a man selling hot dogs right in front of you. He's the one screaming out "hot dogs" (stop judging and fondle his buns!).

Say you're rolling up and down the meat aisle at the grocery store. You spot a single man (hint: they're the ones with 12 boxes of ballpark franks and no toilet paper in their cart). Cut him off by the ketchup and wink at him.

Read the obituaries to find widowers, and start going to funerals. Stand next to him at the grave and whisper in his ear, "I have meatloaf!"

Go anywhere, really (except the bra department at Macys). If you walk outside, you'll see a bunch of men everywhere, grazing, clueless as to where they're going or what they want. Tap them on the shoulder and say, "Look no further, you've found your gal!"

I Don't Know What To Say!

If you see a man in a public place, you can capture his interest by using a little ingenuity in your introduction. "Hi, how are you?" is dull.

Besides, you may get an answer; and the truth is, you don't ever really want to know how anybody really is. If they were to tell you, you'd run. That's one of the main reasons men so often don't tell us their feelings and thoughts. Their inner thoughts would scare the girl right out of us.

The goal of a line is to begin a conversation … not to freak someone out. It's an entrée to a relationship, an invitation to prolong. You want to open with something that sparks a response. "Hi, how are you?" quite often sparks "Fine," and that's the end of it! Everybody's always fine. Always. We might as well add that to the question, "Hi, how are you, fine?"

You'll need something to say, even though you might consider yourself to be generally extremely interesting and witty. You never know when Mr. "Oh, All Right" is right in front of you. Remember, you stink, pee-u at this.   Or else you'd be in a relationship already!

MISSED OPPORTUNITIES ARE LIKE TRAINS. YEAH, THERE MAY BE ANOTHER ONE COMING, BUT THE ONE YOU JUST MISSED WILL GET YOU THERE FASTER, AND PROBABLY HAD BETTER SNACKS.

A great thing to say is, **"Bonjour, Monsieur care for a spanking?"**

That's a conversation starter. This is not an invitation to study. Speak French, any French; they don't understand, but they think it's sexy. Bonjour Monsieur, voulez vous une croissant? O escargot? Une *spanking?* Zsa Zsa Gabor? Vichyssoise? French fries? Une spanking? French, French, French!

BONJOUR MONSIEUR! Voulez vous?

Some Bad 'Hello' Ideas:

- ♥ My, you have shiny hair. I can see my teeth in it.
- ♥ Wanna see a sexy stretch mark?
- ♥ You don't scare me—I've slept with crack addicts.

- ♥ If you take me out and dump me... I'll stalk you.

- ♥ Let's get a drink of something, I have a bladder infection.

- ♥ Can you buy me something? I left my wallet in my previous marriage.

- ♥ Mi vagina no es occupada!

- ♥ I'm two months behind in my rent and there's a boot on my car.

- ♥ Do you know the way to San Jose?

- ♥ Hey, haven't we met? Aren't you in my bipolar therapy group?

WARNING:
THE WRONG KIND OF MAN
IS EVERYWHERE.
A FEW SIMPLE QUESTIONS
CAN VERIFY
THAT HE IS WRONG.
LIKE, "ARE YOU GAY?"

Gay Men Are Not Straight

Gay men are so ridiculously attractive, it just seems cruel! They make great companions. They actually ask you questions about YOU! And then they let you go on and on, much like your girlfriends. It's breathtaking.

And it's hard to believe, I know! They bask you in so much attention, you can't believe they aren't attracted to you. You start thinking, "Yeah, maybe he USED to be gay, but that's just because he hadn't met ME yet. I can change him! NO YOU CAN'T ... no you can't. He's just using you to get to your brother! Gay men don't turn straight as they get older, they turn into older gay men.

Repeat this affirmation with Dr. Zelda:

"I cannot make a gay man straight, no matter how many times I show him my cleavage!"

Many women have asked me, "Zelda, what kind of man does Zelda like?" My answer is simple: **Zelda likes the ones that like Zelda**. Zelda does not believe in unrequited love *(loving someone who loves someone else, or simply does not love you, is just DUMB)*. Spit it out! Bleh! Get over that syndrome. You simply do not want someone who does not want you. Waste of time. Mine, yours, his, your friends'.

WASTE OF TIME... Repeat that, **"It is a waste of time to love someone who does not love me."**

You've heard the phrase, *"If you love someone, set them free, if they don't return, hunt them down and kill them?"*

If a man is meant to be yours, he will be. Find men who like you.

There's even a song about it:

"If you like-a-me, then I like-a-you!"

Remember when you were in first grade and you could walk up to another first grader and say, "I like you, do you want to be my friend?" And they would say "yes" or "no." This technique actually works very well, even today with adults. I have several unattached single girlfriends who sit around lusting after the wrong types: too young, too famous, too handsome, and too married.

Remember, love is relative. You can learn to love anybody.

How To Flirt Without Throwing Out Your Back

Have you ever seen chicki-wahs out in the meet market who are just naturally in touch with their inner sluts? Their inner *trampolina*? They wink without even knowing it? They giggle at every little thing he says. And they get all the men!? They convince men that they are gorgeous, without necessarily being gorgeous!

You must get in touch with your inner slutsky, too. Watch these women. Copy them. They'll walk up to a complete stranger at the Post Office and say, "Hey handsome, you wanna lick my stamps?" They'll stand in the fruit section of the grocery store and fondle the casabas, making eye contact with passerby men and say, "I don't know if these are too hard?"

Practice making goo-goo eyes. Flirt with your girlfriends for practice (maybe you'll even like it).

The Strumpet

Flirting is experiential. The more you do it, the better you get at it.

Speak in whispers, like you're out of breath. Act as if Darth Vader swallowed Marilyn Monroe.

Try to look helpless. Men love helpless chicki-wahs.

Ways to be helpless:

- ♥ Jump into the ocean, swim out beyond the buoys and flap your arms (warning, a few of my followers were not rescued in time).
- ♥ Flatten your tire on the side of a road.
- ♥ Stand on a ladder in a hardware store (any aisle) and tear up.

Pouty lips are always good. Sad little smiles work nicely. If you can work up a tear or two, you are in like Flinterella. Lick your lips often. In fact, let your tongue completely hang out.

BTW: Don't dress slutty. That's just slutty. Make them use their noggins to imagine!

Zelda Teaching Her Very Popular Flirting Technique At Her Workshop "Voulez Voulez?" In Dubuque, Iowa.

Prerequisite: You must have a fifth grade knowledge of French.

Too Old For Love, Or Care For A Kidnapping?

There was once a statistic reported that women over the age of forty have a greater chance of getting kidnapped by a terrorist than of getting married. So, what that basically says is a woman over forty is just too old to even get kidnapped. It's insulting, and it makes the hair on the back of my knees stand up.

After all, a kidnapping is a relationship too! Just ask Patty Hearst! Remember, lower your standards!

Perhaps you'd be better off with a terrorist, anyway. The average terrorist kidnapping lasts twice as long as the average relationship. You wouldn't have to worry where he was nights, he'd wait on you hand and foot, and when it was all over you could sell the story to LIFETIME TELEVISION and make a million dollars. LIFETIME loves movies-of-the-week about kidnappings with happy endings. Jenny Garth would star.

Strange bedfellows are better than no bedfellows at all.

Yes I will sleep with you...
Just please don't speak!

Remember, You Are Never Too Old For Love!

There is a mistaken belief that falling in love doesn't feel as good when you get older. A fluttery stomach is a fluttery stomach.

Giddy is giddy. Happy is happy. Men are still weird.

Repeat this affirmation:

"My skin may not fit me anymore, and my boobs might have begun to meet my ass on the side, but I am still gorgeous" *(to someone with cataracts).*

It is never too late to find love. Here are some places you can cruise older men:

- ♥ ICUs
- ♥ Flomax section of the pharmacy
- ♥ Your best married friend's funeral
- ♥ Early bird dinner specials
- ♥ The jello tray at any dinner buffet
- ♥ Shuffleboard courts

Part III:
So I Got Me One, What Now Zelda?

HOW WEIRD IS REALLY WEIRD?

Okay, so we admit all men are a little weird, but you must make sure your man is within the boundaries of acceptably weird. I mean, there is weird and then there is *weird.*

How to tell if he's really weird:

- 💜 He pulls up in front of your house on a motorized skateboard and skips up to your front door singing 'Zippadee-doo-dah!"

- 💜 He doesn't knock on your door; instead, he stands out front and yells, "Ding-dong!"

- 💜 He calls you "the beef."

- 💜 He tells your roommate that if things don't work out with you, he'll be coming for her next.

Make sure you know how to communicate with this weirdo-alien. Remember, you don't speak the same language. Not only does he not know this, but he does not care. If you tried to explain things to him, he would raise his eyebrow, as if you were speaking another language (which you are). So, stop talking to a wall of *what-the-heck* and learn to relate to and communicate with this person.

It's up to you. How many times must I say it is UP TO YOU!!!???

Warning:

MEN DO NOT SPEAK ENGLISH, THEY SPEAK MANGLISH.

Men are not very good listeners. So, if you have a problem that you'd like to dramatize and turn into an opera (which we chicki-wahs do), *call another chicki-wah.* If your toaster needs a fixin', give it to him. If you have a serious problem about life, do NOT take it to him. He will only be interested for a short time and then move into a fix-it situation. Whereas, the truth is, you just feel like going on and on, and on ... and on ... and on ... and on ... and on ... and on...

(More Manglish in section MEN: THE OTHER WHITE MEAT)

Dating (Or, I'd Rather Get Abducted By Aliens)

The good news is that you HAVE been abducted by an alien. And if all goes well, he will be taking you back to his planet WIERDON, but he will not give you an anal probe (unless you want him to!). However, he will spend his lifetime wondering how you work, what the heckola you're thinking, and what makes you tick, etc. He will never ask, he will just wonder. (That's what those LONG silences are.)

In all seriousness, dating is like shucking raw oysters. You're just going to have to keep shucking until you get one that isn't rancid, and hopefully will come with a pearl! There's no easy way through this process. Just do it. For more information on the dating process, please consult my manual, "DATING AND OTHER UNIMAGINABLE HORRORS." But here's a big hint in the meantime:

Be really, really, really nice on the first couple of dates. In other words, don't be you. Be someone else.

SEX IS LIKE
A BOX OF CHOCOLATES—
SOMETIMES YOU WILL
GET THE GOOEY JELLY ONE.
THOSE ARE JUST THE BREAKS!

The single biggest mistake people make in relationships is jumping into bed too soon with each other. Listen, sisters, I'm from the '70's, an era when you could have sex easier than you could get a pack of bubblegum. All you had to do was say, "Hey, you wanna?" and they'd say, "Yeah."

You'd be standing at a Dunkin Donuts counter one minute, next thing you know you're playing hide the cruller with the counter boy. It was everywhere. This country was like one big **Plato's Retreat (8)**.

You never know what you're going to get with sex. However, no matter which one you get, you should be okay ... unless it's the gooey jelly one, of course. Nobody likes those; why they still make them is beyond Zelda, and I'm a doctor. If you went to the city dump, there would be millions of them sitting around in the bottom of empty boxes of chocolate, each with one bite missing.

REMEMBER, IT'S NOT THAT HARD TO FIND A MAN TO SLEEP WITH YOU. THE HARD PART IS GETTING HIM TO STAY THROUGH COFFEE.

Do not have sex too soon. Women bond during sex. Men do not. You will get attached; he will not. You will get clingy; he will get antsy. You will lose him. Trust me.

In fact, do not have sex until he buys you something ... big, like a *boat.* And after you have sex for the first time, he's gonna wanna know how many men have been there before him. Whatever you do, don't answer that question; it's a trap. If he stupidly asks you if he was the first, just smile and say, "You might have been; you do look familiar."

How To Get A Man To Express His Feelings Without Vomiting

Remember during the romantic era (the early dating process), when he was on his best behavior? He looks into your eyes and tells you what he's thinking, and it's always about YOU!

He very strongly resembles someone with really good communication skills. It's not perfect, but it's nice. He's trying. You call all your girlfriends up and say, "Wow, this one COMMUNICATES! He's REALLY IN TOUCH WITH HIMSELF." Meantime, when he's with his friends who ask him how the date went, he just shrugs. They know what that means; they speak Manglish. It means, 'okay.'

Remember this: the skills he already demonstrated at the beginning are as good as it gets. He doesn't have any better skills than those.

CONSIDER THE DATING PROCESS A COSTCO DEMONSTRATION

When you buy a Costco gadget and bring it home, the end product won't ever taste as good or work as well as it did when the hair-netted lady at the store made it. That handy electric cucumber juice gadget just kind of loses its gleam when you actually start stuffing your own cucumbers in the plastic carafe in your kitchen. Suddenly, you remember you don't even like cucumber juice. Next thing you know, you start planning a garage sale (don't bring a man home just to put him out in a garage sale the next day).

Talking About His Feelings

Your man isn't going to communicate his feelings unless you coach him. It's like a gymnastic event at the Olympics: degree of difficulty, 8.9. He may even need a spotter. We ask for quiet on the deck and we stand arms out-stretched, only intervening if he calls out or gets hurt.

That conversation might go something like this:

SHE: What are you thinking?

HE: Nothing. *(Probably true.)*

SHE: You never speak of your feelings. What do you feel?

HE: I feel like...

SHE: Yes?

HE: I feel like having pizza.

SHE: I mean about me. What do you feel about me?

HE: I feel like you shouldn't have any pizza.

Do be warned that a certain breed of man, when asked about his feelings, and then is coached and prodded ... might begin to vomit years of feelings onto you. He won't stop. It will just keep coming. Like the Exorcist. Yes, it will be green and everything. You will need a mop and a pail. You will eventually say, "SHUT UP." And he will, never to mention a feeling again, except one ... "I feel like having sex."

I'm just saying, this happened to me once.

And remember, when a man says "I don't understand," he isn't saying, "Wow, that's so unfair; I don't understand how that happened to you." He is saying, "I DON'T UNDERSTAND." Or "NO SPEAK DA ENGLISH!" At this point, you can't just repeat yourself. You must figure out another way to say it. Why must YOU do all the work? Because, *Zelda already told you*, he simply doesn't know how. You are woman, hear you roar. You can fry up the bacon and answer a question at the same time. You are a waitress in the breakfast buffet of life.

Getting Some Intimacy
(Or Misery Loves Company)

WARNING:

JUST BECAUSE A MAN LOVES YOU DOES NOT MEAN HE WANTS TO KNOW EVERYTHING ABOUT YOU!

We women do like to blather on about our lives. This is intimacy to us: talking on about extremely personal things that don't need to be repeated. One time I told the grocery store bag man that I was having hot flashes. He began to cry; it was simply too much intimacy for a bagger at Piggly Wiggly.

The unleashing of your inner primordial dreck is NOT bonding. It's annoying. If you continue down this dead end, your man will eventually say, *"Can you try not to have so many feelings in front of me? Don't you have any girlfriends?"*

You've made the mistake of casting your blabber before swine. Call a girlfriend; she's dying to know what's going on over there. The truth is, when you become intimate with a man, you need your girlfriends more than ever to chatter with, so your man doesn't have to listen (because he really doesn't care how uneven your flow was that month). No matter how much of a prince he is, he'll still always be thinking, "Ew." He really doesn't want to know how many hours you spend searching for the perfect under eye concealer. He's not sure what needs to be concealed, and this frightens him. He knows where your eyes are, but that's about the end of his interest. (Honestly, to him, under the eyes means your boobs.)

He also doesn't want to know about your ex-boyfriends, even the ones that beat you— especially the ones that beat you. This does nothing for his erection, and his erection seems to be most of what he's willing to do something for. So shut your pie hole and stay naked. If this seems archaic, and anti-women's lib-ish … tough toenails. It works.

NOW THAT I HAVE IT ALL— WHERE DO I PUT HIM?

Having it all is not all it's cracked up to be. Remember all those coupled girlfriends of yours who always warned you (unprovoked),

"Relationships are A LOT OF WORK?" Well, that's an understatement.

 So, now there's a man in your bed, in your home, in your stuff, in your head, in your dreams, in your fears. Get over it. Love can be scary. I told you to make sure you wanted this! Things will be different from here on out.

HAVING A BOYFRIEND IS LIKE PUTTING ON LIPSTICK WITH NO HANDS. IT TAKES LUCK, LOTS OF CONCENTRATION, AND A VERY SUPPORTIVE TEAM AROUND YOU.

I'm In Love ... I Think?

So, you think maybe, possibly, there's a chance that you're in love. How do you know for sure? That's the biggest fear we all have (besides trying on bathing suits at Macy's).

BTW – they use skinny mirrors at Macy's, so be warned. You don't look as good as they present. They should put a

disclaimer on the mirror, "Warning, objects may be larger than they appear." But I digress...

Firstly and mostly... Do not confuse LUST with LOVE.

LUST IS NOT LOVE
ANY MORE THAN
A HAMBURGER
AT MCDONALD'S IS BEEF

Some Signs You Might Be In Love:

- ♥ If it feels a little bit like you have to throw up, that is love (or bulimia).
- ♥ If you have lost your appetite, that is love (or the flu).
- ♥ If you doodle his name all over your things, that is love (or insanity or both).
- ♥ If you find yourself slipping his name into every conversation you have with anyone, that is love.
- ♥ If you drive by his house on your way to the corner grocery store, (but he lives on the other side of town), that is not love. That is called stalking.

TRUE LOVE MEANS NOBODY WILL EVER HURT YOU AGAIN, EXCEPT HIM.

There's no feeling like falling in love. When you have fallen, you want to call every girlfriend you have. You want to tell her every little detail of how he told you. You want them all to know how much he loves you. It's not enough that YOU know, now EVERYONE must know. You take out an ad in the local paper. You have a party. You invite everyone over to meet Mr. Right – now.

- ♥ **You can tell he loves you** if you wake up in the morning and *he's staring at you like he's going to eat you.*

- ♥ **You can tell he loves you** if you go to sleep at night and *he's staring at you like he's going to eat you.*

The Hardest Part About Falling In Love Is The Beginning Part. Whom Tells Whom First?

If someone tells you they love you, and you are either not sure how you feel, or know you don't love him too ... be very careful what flies out of your mouth. It could ruin your man for the next chicki-wah he tangos with (and that could be ... uhm ... ME!). So, treat him as you would have him treat you. Give him chocolate! And whatever you do, do NOT say one of the following things:

- ♥ Well, that's gonna cost you.
- ♥ Thank you!
- ♥ Do you know the way to San Jose?
- ♥ I speaka no English!

There are really no hard and fast Zelda rules about when it's appropriate to tell someone you love them. You will know when it's time. You will feel like you're going to explode if you don't. It might just fall out of your mouth one day.

BTW: If he says it first, it may sound suspiciously like a burp. Don't be frightened; he is doing the best he can.

He Loves Me, Yuck!
(Be Careful What You Wish For!)

Okay, so he loves you. In fact, he loves you so much you are sick. You're scared. Whatever you want to do, he says, "That's fine, Snookums. Whatever makes you happy. I just want to be with you for my entire life, by your side, holding your hand, reading your thoughts, taking in your breath, suffocating you... Until you die."

He wants to get adjoining nose piercings, with a ring that attaches you together; it's sickening. People make that "finger down the throat" gag gesture when you walk in a room, arm-in-arm, and glittering eyeballs to glittering eyeballs. Even your mother is sick of your happiness. She asks you how it's possible for someone to love you so much. I mean, "you're nice and all," she says, "but really? Who is this guy"?

Enjoy this phase, as it will not last. The good news is that your lonely nights are over. The bad news is that your alone nights are over. He came for the sex, but he's staying for the food. Do be sure to feed him.

Is This Mr. Right?

We all fear that we are with the wrong man-eo. We all fear that our love isn't strong enough, good enough, right enough, hot enough, and on and on. Everyone else's looks so much better. The grass is always greener!

How do I know its love? How long does it last? Where does it go when it goes?

Does true love last, or does it melt like a bowl of ice cream leaving a big ring around the bowl, which reminds you the next morning how many reckless calories you shoved down your gullet last night during a weak moment? *(I will be discussing this and many other run-on sentences in the final chapter of my opus.)*

I personally believe true love cannot die. It can morph into something else, but true love is alive, and like cockroaches, it's really hard to kill.

How do you know when love is over? Don't worry about love dying a violent and sudden death; if it does, you can't do anything about it. I probably shouldn't have even brought it up. Seriously, I shouldn't have.

You can be in love, stay in love, live in love, dwell in love, and linger in love ... **if you want**. You are not a dish of mold; you have choices. But love takes work. And it will be up to you to do most of the work. Why? You are not paying attention ... because your man is not aware that it takes work.

After the initial love haze blows off and flies away, you are left with a Mr. Man. You need more qua ... which is what Dr. Zelda is going to speak about in the next section of this manual.

I Know We Just Met Today, But Can I Move In Tomorrow?

So you two have decided to move in together! Congratulations! Have I used too many exclamation points?!?!?!? I'm excited for you. This is huge. To think ... your rent is about to be cut in HALF. This is as good a reason as any to move in with your man-boy.

But, the first and most important thing to remember is that you must set boundaries immediately.

WARNING:

THERE'S A MAN IN YOUR HOUSE!
ARE YOU READY TO GIVE UP
THE DRAWER SPACE?

Make sure you move into YOUR HOUSE, so you are STILL THE BOSS. The House Frau! The Domestic Goddess. The Countess of the Casa!

This is very important. I don't care if he has a mansion, and you live in the dumpster behind your mother's house. Either he moves in with you, or he buys you a new place to move into together, so you can maintain control.

The Queen's Rules

Who is the master of the house? Why, you are, chicki-wah! So, the rules are whatever you say they are at any given moment. Yes, they can change. The minute he learns them, you switch it all on him again, just to keep him on his toes. You might not be aware you're doing this, but it is written that you may.

So ... his **Weed Whacker** goes in the garage, along with most of his things. He gets one sock drawer and the whole garage, which he must keep clean. When his friends come over, this is where they shall hang. They may each come in ONCE to use the bathroom during one of these 'hangs.' Sometime around 10ish, you will open the door to the garage and nicely say, "Honey, it's time your little friends went home, don't you think?"

**BE VERY CAREFUL
WHICH SIDE OF THE BED YOU CHOOSE...
THIS COULD BE FOR THE REST OF YOUR
LIFE. HE WILL NEVER SWITCH WITH YOU
(UNLESS YOU ARE DYING, MAYBE).**

His snowshoes are NOT wall art. His poster from the Indianapolis 500 is not going on any wall in your home. Even if it doesn't have thumbtack holes in it, it's not living room material. The pictures of his girlfriends (even the ones from kindergarten) are to be de-framed and put away. Your pictures of your ex-boyfriends are to be left around as warnings.

So you think you are done?!

Think again ... you are just beginning!

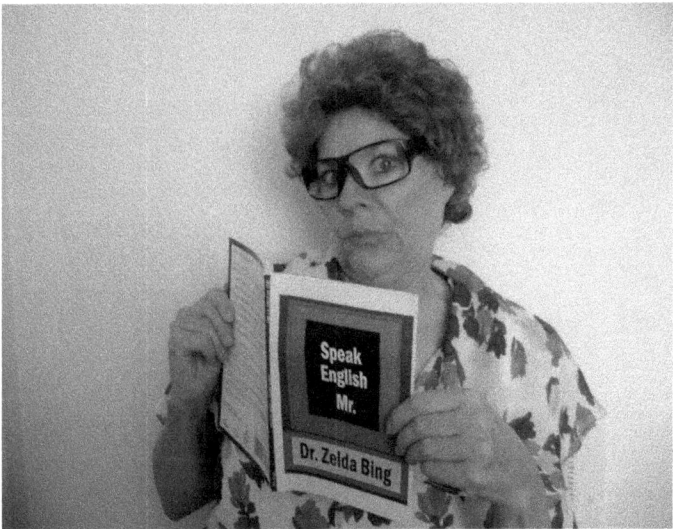

Part IV:
Men: The Other White Meat –
The Ongoing Manual –
The Manual That Goes On And
On ... And On ... And On...

I Can't Go On! You Must Go On!

When you buy any item, you get a manual for ongoing care. When you buy garments, they have care tags. "Wash in warm water and wring dry." Or, "Take to a professional."

Even CHEERIOS has directions on the box. It tells you to put them in a bowl, pour milk onto them and eat with a spoon (this technique works okay on men too, FYI). But, in all cerealness, what do we really know about the maintenance schedule of a man?

For example, do you know...

- ♥ When to feed him?
- ♥ What to feed him?
- ♥ When to sex him?
- ♥ What to sex him?
- ♥ How to make him think he's happy?
- ♥ What the heck is he talking about?
- ♥ What size batteries?
- ♥ How to get rid of him?

MEN ARE LIKE REAL ESTATE. YOU GOTTA KNOW WHEN TO BUY, WHEN TO SELL, AND WHEN TO FLIP.

So let's get to the part where you find out how the heckarooney to relate to, speak to, and hold onto your man.

Remember this; *my opinions are not opinions, they are facts!*

Que Sera Syndrome

Okie dokie, fanokie, so now you are living with a man, or something that strongly resembles one; and if this goes well, you will get married! Or, if things go well, you will break up... Only time will tell which one of these things will be better for you. Things have a way of happening as they should. I truly believe in the power of *what is meant to be **will** be*. Que Sera, Sera. Whatever will be, will be. *Let it be.* It's the Que Sera Sera Syndrome. So, let it be.

91

Trust me, everything you need to know about men, you can find in the title of a pop song. Songs like "Easy to Be Hard," "People are Strange," and "She Wore An Itsy Bitsy Teeny Weenie Yellow Polka Dot Bikini."

GETTING MARRIED Or Till Death Do We Part - *How Much Longer Will That Be Exactly?*

Say the question was popped, and you are going to get married. You're going to the Chapel of Love. I wish you nothing but good luck. You will need it. Many marriages break up during the planning of the nuptials alone!

I, myself, have been married five times (and for those of you who are counting, yes ... I got married one more time during the creating of this MANUAL). I think this one is going to stick. He's not going anywhere; he lost his driver's license. The sad but true factoid is that 50% of all marriages fail. Most people don't do the work. A marriage is just a relationship with no end in sight.

QUITE OFTEN,
WHEN THE GOING GETS TOUGH,
THE TOUGH GET THE HECK
OUTTA THERE.

You might want to purchase my manual on getting married:

By The Way... I've Rented You A Tux, What Are You Doing Next Saturday?

And staying married:

What? Are You Still Here?

Mr. & Miss-Communication -
If You Don't Understand Each Other, You Have a Better Chance of Staying Together

Man has been around since the dawn of man. Women came right after or right before, or maybe at the exact same time. Who really gives a Horton's hoot who came first; the man, the woman, the chicken, the egg, or Larry King? The real question is, "Since we've all been around so darn long, how come we still don't know what in tarnation the other is talking about?"

Believe me, it could be worse, but it isn't very good. For example, if communication were left up to the men, we'd still be grunting and pointing when we liked something. You can still see leftovers of this behavior during sporting events. Sometimes it's evident even while they're eating, and have a full mouth, but still feel the need to speak, or ask for seconds. I mean, here they are with a full frontal load, and they're still grunting and pointing ... as if they could even fit one more thing down that gullet!!!

**MY BOYFRIEND AND I
DON'T SPEAK THE SAME
LAUNGUAGE
AT ALL.
HE'S SICILIAN
AND I'M THIN CRUST.**

Fortunately, several thousand years ago, we women took control of the communication.

A Brief Herstory of Communication
CAVE MEN are MEN, TOO!

The first words ever spoken by man were actually said by a woman, and it was a shrug (sometime around the year 9,000 B.C.). Almost fifty years later, she came up with the "hmmm," followed by an eye roll; then, she eventually evolved that "hmmm" into a fully voiced "ahem." It was loaded with that attitude women are so good at.

Man responded for the first time about a century later. He worked for decades on his response and finally eked out, "Is something wrong, dear?" This question remains a staple in man's limited communication repertoire. (To him, up means 'yes,' down means 'no.') "Is something wrong, dear?" was the perfect opening for us chicki-wahs to tell him!

"What's wrong? What's _not_ wrong? I'm cold, I'm sick of this boar's hide dress – mastodon tartare for dinner every single night – you left the toilet rock up – blah blah blah – Are you serious? What's _not_ wrong?"

Woman just shrugged and rolled her eyes up into her head (this would become her 'go-to') and said, "Nothing." In truth, she wanted her he-man to know, without asking. Women have this eternal need to be understood, so the desire to have people fish for answers began. This was also the beginning of men and women not having a clue what the other wanted or how to give it to them.

YES, EVER SINCE THE DAWN OF MAN, MEN WERE THE HUNTERS, WOMEN WERE THE HINTERS.

THE FIRST FIGHT

Two Newlyweds sometime around 9,000 B.C. (Before **C**omplaining**).**

CAVE WOMAN: Ahem...

CAVE MAN: Is something wrong, dear?

CAVE WOMAN: Uhm...

CAVE MAN: Okay, then bye.

A year later she spoke again.

CAVE WOMAN: Uhm...

CAVE MAN: Yes dear? What is it?

CAVE WOMAN: Nothing.

CAVE MAN: Then I'm going to go shuffle rocks with Clack.

CAVE WOMAN: Well...

CAVE MAN: Well, what?

CAVE WOMAN: Never mind *(eye roll)*.

CAVE MAN: Okay, that works for me.

CAVE WOMAN: Weeeeeeeeeeeee...

CAVE MAN: What is it?

CAVE WOMAN: I'm hungry. And I'm cold. And I'm bored out of my gourd (which I just ate, by the way). If only there were something I could watch all day ... say a little electronic box that showed pictures of other people's lives, with sound.

CAVE MAN: Sorry.

A year later she spoke again.

CAVE WOMAN: I'm leaving you.

CAVE MAN: Well, I'm not surprised; you've been bitching since the late 9,000's.

CURTAIN

So, could Zelda Bing parlez-vous that verbal communication evolved out of the women's eternal need to complain? Yes she could. And I will, with great glee!

And it's a good thing! If cave women didn't complain, we'd all still be sitting on pointy boulders, showering with elephant trunks, and speaking through a wooly mammoth tusk phone. It's a good thing we chicki-wahs took the initiative to complain, prod, suggest, whine, and roll those eyes. This is called communication.

But, maybe if she'd just come right out and given him a direct answer somewhere around the year ... oh say ... 5,000 B.C., we'd be better at communication by now. We wouldn't have to complain or hint to get our points across. Perhaps?

NO
COMPLAIN,
No Gain!

We women believe that complaining is the mother's milk of a relationship. We like to slurp it up daily. It is our innermost primal need crying out to be heard. It's how we bond with other women, so we try to bond with men like this too! This is our big boo-boo. It's like mowing your lawn with a hair dryer. You are mixing metaphors. (Or am I? I'm not sure which of us is mixing!)

To this day, men do not care for women's complaining. They call it "bitching."

Men think complaining is annoying. Truth is, complaining _is_ annoying.

NOBODY REALLY LIKES A COMPLAINER. NOT EVEN OTHER COMPLAINERS.

Complainers are the ones who complain the most about people complaining to them. It's kind of weird. But Zelda digresses.

So how do we bond with men? Back off! I'm getting to that.

How To Speak Manglish

And BTW: That is the eternal, age-old question. Geeze Louise, whoever gets that question right, goes right to DOUBLE JEOPARDY. They win the NOBEL PEACE PRIZE and a LIVE-IN MAID FOR LIFE.

Women simply do not hear things the way men say them. Let's face it, men and women have different sets of ears and mouths. Words fly out of a male's mouth, take a u-turn, change meaning, and dawdle on over to the female's ears. By the time it gets to the woman's ears, she's already moved onto another topic. Plus, men don't hear anything women say, period.

For example, if you say to your man, "never mind," he will NEVER MIND. He takes things literally. He might even wait a full century before he minds again. Or, he may never mind again for the rest of eternity.

And here it is 5,000 years later, and we're still saying, "nothing's wrong," when something is clearly wrong. Women seem to like to make men fish in our mind-ponds to figure out what's wrong. Somehow that would make it all the more sweet. But when we say, "nothing is wrong," he's still responding with something like, "okay then, we'll see ya. I'm goin' fishing with the boys."

WHEN A MAN GOES FISHING, HE LIKES TO CATCH SOMETHING BESIDES AN ATTITUDE.

Men don't speak English. They may speak Manglish, but we chicki-wahs are no better. We speak **Hintglish.** We women don't communicate as well as we think we do, either. We hint. We beat around the bush. We roll our eyes. We make 'tsk' sounds, and we speak to our friends instead of our men.

Maybe its time we got off our high dinosaur and learned to speak Manglish. Why is it OUR responsibility, chicki-wahs? Because we're the ones crying out to connect, through hints. He's the one hunting for something to eat. At the end of the day, we'll be whining and he'll be dining!

GETTING A MAN TO
SPEAK ABOUT HIS FEELINGS
IS LIKE EATING CHICKEN NOODLE SOUP
WITH YOUR HANDS.
YOU HAVE TO MOVE FAST,
OR IT ALL JUST SLIPS
THROUGH YOUR FINGERS.

Getting a man to speak about his feelings is a chore, like washing windows. You'll put it off for weeks, months, even seasons; and when you finally get to it, you will see things so clearly. You'll wish you had done it years ago.

When the man does attempt to eke a feeling out, it may sound strange. Sometimes it sounds like he has a hairball stuck in his throat ... he'll start gagging on the attempt. You may even have to hit him hard on the back to get it out. Zelda has been known to perform the Heimlich maneuver on a man who had a feeling stuck on his epiglottis.

The Feeling Fiasco

HER: What are you feeling?

HIM: I feel ... I feeeeeeeel ... I feel like having sex.

HER: That's not a feeling.

HIM: It sure feels like one.

HER: How do you feel about me?

HIM: I don't feel like having sex with *you. I want sex with your roommate.*

Manglish To Hintglish Translation:

As you may have surmised by now, it takes a lifetime to become fluent at Manglish. But, the following translation tips will at least get you started, and keep you safe in a storm.

When A Man Says:

"DID YOU SAY SOMETHING?"

(Translation: I don't just mean this minute, I mean since we met, because I haven't been listening.)

"DID YOU JUST SAY SOMETHING?"
(Translation: I haven't been listening at all, but I have particularly not been listening this last hour.)

"I WASN'T THINKING ABOUT ANYTHING."
(Translation: He wasn't thinking about anything. It's actually possible for a man; so for the love of candy, stop prodding him.)

"I'LL GET TO IT LATER."
(Translation: Do it yourself.)

"OF COURSE I'M LISTENING."
(Translation: Would you shut up already!)

"WHAT'S FOR DINNER?"
(Translation: You are not being taken out; you are cooking.)

"PUT ON WHATEVER TV SHOW YOU WANT TO WATCH."
(Translation: I'll be asleep in a minute.)

"SO, HOW DID YOUR DAY GO?"
(Translation: Go ahead and talk now, so I can have some quiet later.)

"YES, WE CAN DO THAT SOMETIME, JUST NOT NOW."
(Translation: Forget about it.)

"THANKS FOR YOUR HELP, BUT I KNOW WHERE I'M GOING."
(Translation: I don't know where I'm going, but shut your pie hole just the same!)

"I WAS JUST ABOUT TO TAKE CARE OF THAT."
(Translation: I have no memory of saying I would do that.)

"I'D LOVE TO SEE A CHICK FLICK."
(Translation: I'd like to have sex tonight.)

When A Woman Says:

"GIVE ME A MINUTE!"
(Translation: GIVE ME AS MUCH TIME AS I NEED, which I can't at this particular point in time say how much that is; so you can just sit down and wait. And whatever you do, don't turn the TV on.)

"PLEASE DON'T ASK ME THAT AGAIN."
(Translation: Please don't ask her that again. Ever).

"WHATEVER."
(Translation: "OMG, are you a moron?" Why am I even still standing here?)

"YOU DON'T HAVE TO PAY."

(Translation: You have to pay. Whatever, whenever. Just pull out your stash and pay, mister. And don't EVER let this awkward moment happen again. Seriously. Where are you from, Mars?)

"WE CAN WATCH WHATEVER YOU WANT."

(Translation: You can choose from Lifetime, CUTE PUPPIES ON PARADE, The Hallmark Channel, or OWN. Don't make the fatal mistake of straying off this list. It will cost you sex, and a lot of it.)

"I'LL BE OFF THE PHONE IN A MINUTE."

(Translation: Find something to do. I'm going to be on for a while, my friends and I actually talk and listen.)

"I'M JUST GOING TO LOOK AROUND IN THIS STORE FOR A MINUTE."

(Translation: Sit down on the lonely man chair they have placed for you in the mall, and shut up.)

"I'LL BE READY IN A MINUTE."

(Translation: Everything makes me look fat.)

"SURE. YOU CAN HAVE YOUR FRIENDS OVER TO WATCH THE GAME IF YOU HAVE NO OTHER PLACE TO GO."
(Translation: Why here? There are sports bars EVERYWHERE!)

"SOMEONE COULD USE A SHAVE."
(Translation: You're not getting near me with that cheese-grater face.)

"OKAY. WE CAN GO SEE AN ACTION MOVIE TONIGHT."
(Translation: We're not having sex tonight.)

Questions From My Readers & Followers

How do you like your men? I like my men like I like my coffee: hot, strong, and served with a donut. I like my men like I like my cheese: hard, stinky, and from France.

Do men think about us as much as we think about them? Yes, but it doesn't feel like a thought. It feels like a boner.

Why don't men like to talk about their feelings? It gets in the way of their boner!

How do you know if it's been too long since you've had sex? If a dog starts to hump your leg, and you don't stop him, it's been too long.

Do you use a vibrator? Absolutely, they're really good for your teeth.

What's your favorite position, and why? #48, because it's close to #49. I also like the pizza defensive.

How do you know when it's time to have sex? It's time whenever the woman says it's time. Not a second before.

Why do men always argue with everything? Because they're always wrong, and wrong people are irritated, and irritation causes arguments (and rashes!).

How do you keep your sex life alive? I water it.

> If all
> else fails...
> I always have
> CANDY!

Happily Ever After, And Other Fairy Tales

That's just a catchy title. I'm sorry, but there really isn't a happily ever after. You aren't Cinderella for Pete's sake! There's just life on life's terms. Relationships have their ups and downs, ins and outs, overs and outs, thicks and thins. Then you will get to the first anniversary. And it all begins again.

Besides, happiness is overrated and underappreciated. People who are naturally happy, take it for granted. Those who are never happy think the people who are always happy are lying.

So, how do you know if you're happy? Look at your face in the mirror; if its smiley, then you're probably happy (or you're a phony, and only you know which it is).

Look around, if all your friends are sick of you and your happiness, then you might be happy. If a complaining girlfriend is suddenly annoying, you might have moved into Happytown, a very nice place where negative complaining energy is annoying.

You might be happy if you no longer eat a quart of ice cream every night to fill the empty hole.

You might be happy if your heart skips a little beat every time you lay your eyes on your man. Embrace your happiness. Give it a hug. Enjoy! Don't worry about the 50% divorce rate. Seriously, don't ... I shouldn't have brought it up *(again)*.

So, now your relationship is in your hands. Remember, you are the MATING BUTLER. It is your responsibility. Why? Because he doesn't care. He doesn't even know the darn thing needs butlering. It's a daily cleanup job. There are ashtrays to empty, toilets to bleach, and beer stains on your sofa.

I have to leave you now to manage your relationship so I can go and tend to mine. Oh, I'm not just a doctor ... I am a client.

Remember ... love the one you're with. If you need further training in finding happiness, get my new book,

"I'm Going To Shove This Happy Into You Whether You Want It Or Not."

It will be available soon.

Good luck. You're done with your training. Put on your wheels and roll on! Go on! Scat!

Remember: love yourself—just not in front of anybody.

ZELDA BING (as in DOCTOR Zelda Bing)

Glossary of "Zelda-isms"

(1) Je-nay-say-qua—*I don't know.*

(2) Qua—*Again, I don't know, but I have some.*

(3) Chicki-wah—*Anyone who is out on the hunt.*

(4) Mating Butlers—*You are, dear.*

(5) Garcinia Cambogia—*Another stupid weight loss product that doesn't work.*

(6) ZELF—*A medical term, that's a combo of SELF & ZEST.*

(7) MOO-GOO-GAI-PAN—*A Chinese chicken dish that I enjoy.*

(8) PLATO'S RETREAT—*A gawdy buffet of sexual permissiveness. Situated in NYC, in the 70's. So tawdry that even Zelda only went two or three times. (Five times, tops).*

About the Author

Debbie Kasper is an award winning performer, emmy nominated writer, stand-up comedian, actress, international humor author, essayist, director, producer, and coach.

She has written for several TV shows, including the seminal shows; Roseanne and *The Rosie O'Donnell Show*. Her one woman show *Without Me, My Show Is Nothing* received the distinguished Drama-Logue award for "Best One-Person Show in LA." Her book *Bras and Penus on a Date* (a parody of John Gray's *Mars and Venus on a Date*) which she co-wrote, has been translated into several languages and published on four continents. Her essays have appeared in two collections; *No Kidding*, and *Moms Are Nuts*, and have also been featured on several online magazines, including DAME.

Debbie is also a well-known veteran comedian and has performed for colleges, clubs, cruise ships, corporate events, and recovery shows.

Boomermania: The Musical About the Baby Boomers, which she created, wrote, directed and produced with partner Pat Sierchio, is about to launch on a national tour as well. Debbie also toured extensively with, *Self-Help: The Comedy* which she co-wrote with comedian Sheila Kay. Her current one-woman show, starring Zelda Bing; *The Zelda Bing Experience* has premiered on both coasts and is heading for your town.

Please visit my websites:

DebbieKasper.com

ZeldaBing.com

Visit us on facebook, and check out Zelda's

web series on You Tube –

"Zelf-Help with Zelda"

All rights reserved

Cool Jerk Publishing, 2015

That's all folks!